Grace's Adventure

Christine Blake

Grace's Adventure

Copyright © 2024 Christine Blake.

The right of Christine Blake to be identified as the author of this work has been asserted by her in accordance with the Copyright, Designs, and Patents Act 1988.

The author guarantees all contents are original and do not infringe upon the legal rights of any other person or work. All rights reserved. No part of this publication may be reproduced or transmitted in any form or by any means, electronic or mechanical, including photocopy, recording, or any information storage and retrieval system, without permission in writing from the author.

The views expressed in this book are solely those of the author and do not necessarily reflect the views of the publisher, and the publisher hereby disclaims any responsibility for them.

ISBN: 978-1-0687248-2-4

Published by Sunesis Ministries
Website: www.stuartpattico.com

Illustrations by Christine Blake and edited by Bacall Cunningham.

Foreword

I am inspired by God to tell stories about Grace who is a girl that loves God. Grace also sees the world in a humorous way and wants to do the right thing. This story was written to help children to live out their faith in Jesus in their daily lives. To be able to follow the teaching of the 10 Commandments. These humorous stories and amusing characters help children to define their values and character to be great ambassadors in society.

I thank the Lord Jesus Christ who has inspired and shown me that I have destiny and purpose. Thank you for your love, support, and protection. I cannot thank you enough. I thank my husband who I love so much, for his love and support he is a gift from God.

I would like to thank my parents who did their best to bring us up to revere God, from whom I get my values. To my sisters and brothers, you have supported, loved me and been a blessing in my life, thank you I

Love you all. My sister friends you are virtuous women. You lift me up and plant life words in me, God bless you all.

My Niece Bacall who is an inspired artist that did the edits on my Illustrations. My Aunt who taught me how to pray until the power of God comes down. My Pastors who taught me the word of God, how to live by the teachings in the Bible and inspired me. My care group sisters you have lifted me up and been a blessing in my life, thank you and love you much.

Foreword (Gina Lewis) Bachelor of Arts, MSC Social Work, BA English, Master of Science

I have known the author Christine for many years. I was asked to read Graces Adventures and to give my opinion of the book. I found it very comforting reading this book. The interaction between Grace and Percival the frog is multifaceted. They converse about faith in God. They discuss Percival's concerns about his appearance. Grace and Percival identify the things that make them different and unique. Their travels to Jamaica to see the beauty and understand the culture of that land gives children insight about a country different from their own.

All in all, this is a great book and I can envision children enjoying reading it very much.

Important note to parents this statement must be read with your children as it contains a fictitious encounter with a snake. Some snakes can be poisonous extremely dangerous and this book is not encouraging children to tackle snakes if they see one, they should run away and let an adult know what they have seen. The adult will telephone the right authorities who are trained to deal with snakes. Snakes are very dangerous and some have venom that is poisonous and they can bite you.

Grace was woken by the sunlight beaming through her curtains, which warmly caressed her face. Grace got up and peeped through the window and saw it was a beautiful sunny day. She remembered it was Saturday, and there was no school today which made her smile.

The sky was a beautiful cerulean blue with very little clouds, this was the answer to her prayer. Grace believed that if you prayed God answered prayers. It was a perfect day for a picnic so she quickly had a bath and got ready for the day, putting on her favourite dungarees. After breakfast Grace asked "Daddy can I go for a paddle in the brook? it's hot today."

Her father said "Yes Grace, go ahead I will be there soon and I will bring my fishing rod, it's a perfect day for fishing." "I will pack a picnic for you" said her mother, and she packed Graces bag with sandwiches, some crisp sweet apples, and a bottle of homemade delicious lemonade.

Grace decided to take her pet dog named Lisa with her. Grace put a lease around her neck and set off to the brook. The grass was lush and green and in the distance the water was sparkling. Grace knew she would paddle her feet in the cool water.

Grace walked to the brook and when she came to the bank, she laid down on the grass. There were butterflies fluttering around and tiny fish flashed by in the water. Grace decided to stare at the clouds one looked like a ship and the other looked like a giant whale.

She suddenly heard a groaning sound and as she sat up and looked around, she saw a large green frog sitting on a rock in the brook. Grace watched the frog with calm interest, looking at his mouth which was turned down in an unhappy scowl.

"Hello frog, are you ok?" asked Grace, the frog said "my names Percival and it's none of your business." Percival's bad manners upset grace and she also noticed that he was staring at her toes hungrily. Grace looked at him her mouth wide open, "that was so rude," said Grace. Percival poked his tongue out at her and turned his back.

Grace decided to ignore Percival and dangle her feet in the water, it was cool and refreshing on her feet.

Graces attention was caught by a glint of colour in the grass, as it got closer, she realised it was a snake. The snake glided into the water and it was getting closer to where Percival was sitting. Percival could not see the snake because he had his back to it. "Percival, there's a," said Grace. But before she could complete her words he shouted "leave me alone" "But" said Grace, "leave me alone," shouted Percival. With horror Grace saw that the snake was almost upon Percival, at that moment Percival turned around and saw the snake near to him; eyes wide, he croaked and suddenly fainted. Grace said "please Jesus Percival needs your help" she looked around and saw a large stone that fit her hand perfectly. Grace picked up the stone and quickly threw it at the snake, it hit the snake in the centre of its head, and immediately it stopped moving and disappeared under the water.

"Thank you, Jesus," said Grace. Grace picked up Percival and moved to a safe place far away from the snake, Percival woke up shaking with fear and said "you saved me." "No Jesus did, he guided the stone as I threw it, without his help I would not have been so accurate." said Grace

"Next time pay attention when someone speaks to you and don't be so rude," "Yes" said Percival "It doesn't pay to be rude, I'm sorry for being rude to you, I was in a bad mood."

"Why are you in a bad mood Percival"? Grace asked, "because, I'm stuck here in this place and I want to travel and have adventures" he said. "So, what is stopping you Percival?" asked Grace. "Well, I wouldn't survive very long out there without water and you saw what happened with that snake it's not very safe," said Percival.

"Okay, I can see why; but do you know what I do when I want to travel?" "What do you do? asked Percival." "Well," said Grace, "I just lie down, close my eyes, and imagine that I am in the place that I want to be. I will show you, where would you like to go now?" asked Grace. "A beach in Jamaica always wanted to go there and swim in the sea," said Perceval. "Okay, let's go," said Grace. Grace and Percival arrived in Montego Bay in Jamaica. The sun was hot and shining on their skin and the warm golden sand was under their feet. "Percival, what do you see"? asked Grace. "I see blue skies and a man selling coconut's, it is beautiful here" replied Percival.

"Look Grace, I am taller than I was, I must have grown, I won't get eaten by a snake." "Yes, you are taller " said Grace. Percival waved his hands and jumped up and down with excitement.

They soon became aware of soft melodious reggae music that filled the air and a gentle murmur almost like a heartbeat filled Percival with joy. That is Jamaica's Heart, I can feel it he said. "Yes, I feel it too," said Grace as they smiled at each other. "Have you ever had coconut water fresh from a coconut Percival?" "No, ok let's go buy one" said Percival, and they both walked over to the smiling coconut seller as he expertly cut off the top of the coconut with a quick swipe. "Wow said Percival it tastes so refreshing and sweet like nectar." "Yes, it's so good," said Grace.

After finishing their coconut water, Grace and Percival ran down to the sea. As the warm soft water shimmered around them, they dived, swam and raced each other roaring with laughter and filling their hearts with pure joy.

After a long swim, Grace and Percival laid down on the sand. The hot sun quickly dried Graces swimming costume. That was so much fun said Percival, "Yes like swimming in a warm bath," said Grace. "Percival what would you like to do next?" "I would like to climb a waterfall," announced Percival. "Oh, they have one in Ochi Rios named Dunns River Falls," said Grace. "Close your eye's Percival, Its beautiful and near the beach." Percival closed his eyes and when he opened them, he saw a tall waterfall with water cascading down from many levels and he could not stop smiling.

As they looked up there was already a line of people climbing the large rocks. Grace and Percival joined them. The guide said "be careful as you climb up and join hands with your partner." Grace and Percival decided to join them. The view was breath taking and Grace had butterflies in her stomach as she peered down below. The water fell onto their skin and was cool and refreshing. Up and up, they climbed until they got to the top and smiling and breathless, they paddled in the small pool of water.

"Hurray we did it, Percival," shouted Grace. After a short rest they made their way back down.

I wonder what we should do next said Percival, as he wondered the melodious beat of Reggae music filled the air. Grace threw her hands in the air with joy and said "let's dance Percival", "I don't know how to," said Percival sadly. "I'm going to teach you how to do the Jamaican Shuffle, like my Grandad taught me," said Grace. "Put your right foot in front of your left foot and slide your left foot forward and twist your heels like this."

Percival slowly followed the dance steps and then Grace said "Percival you have got the movement right, now let's go faster" as she twisted her body from side to side. Grace and Percival kept dancing until they were tired. "Let us rest now" replied Percival and in agreement they sat down on the beach. "I enjoyed learning the Shuffle and I will teach it to the other frogs," said Percival.

After their rest Grace said "Percival it's time to go back home now, how was your trip?" "The best time I ever had but I miss my pond; perhaps home is not so bad after all and now I can travel to any place with you

Grace," said Percival. Grace replied "You can also read books Percival; I can borrow you my travel books and we can go on adventures together!"

Percival and Grace arrived at the Brook, smiling and happy about their time spent in Jamaica.

"Did you have a good time Percival?" asked Grace. "Yes, I had the best time of my life, going to Jamaica was one of my dreams." said Percival. "I really had a great time and my memories of Jamaica will always make me smile," said Grace.

"Would you like to have some sandwiches and some lemonade"? asked Grace. "Yes please" said Percival and they both munched happily and drank the delicious cool lemonade.

After eating their sandwiches Grace and Percival sat down on the grass, Grace was in deep thought and spoke.

"Percival I just thought of a poem." "Oh, I would like to hear it," said Percival.

Poem in Jamaican Patois
(Jamaican language)

Wan lickle froggy did a sidung eena ah stream
Mi did si di froggy staring at mi feet
Mi seh frog wah mek yaah stare at mi feet"?
Dem a nah flies fi yuh tuh nyam
Dem nar no fly fe you to nyam.

Poem in English

One little frog was sitting in a stream
I saw the frog staring at my feet
I said "frog why are you staring at my feet"
They are not flies for you to eat
They are not flies for you to eat

Grace and Percival looked at each other and fell on the grass, laughter rang out into the air. Percival said to Grace "you know it is not great to be green and to be a frog," "why do you say that Percival," asked Grace. "Well, I am different from other people and the green stands out too much."

Grace replied "I think that God made you the way you look for a reason, and the green helps you to blend in to your surroundings at the brook. Your eyes are great, they see in the front at the sides and partially behind. The only reason you did not see the snakes was because you were in a bad mood. Your green skin also helps to keep you safe and your great fun to be with."

Percival thought for a while and said "You have some good points; I am an excellent swimmer as well." "Yes you are, celebrate yourself" Grace said smiling.

Percival questioned "who is this God anyway"? "Your creator," said Grace. "Green skin, he must have a sense of humour" said Percival and Grace laughed.

"When should we meet again?" asked Percival, "how about next Saturday for 10.00am at the brook?" replied Grace. "Yes, that's a great idea," Percival responded.

They both went happily home.

The End.

www.ingramcontent.com/pod-product-compliance
Lightning Source LLC
Chambersburg PA
CBHW041437010526
44118CB00002B/101